What is the President's Job?

By Allison Singer

US Senior Editor Shannon Beatty
Project Editors Caryn Jenner, Arpita Nath
Project Art Editor Yamini Panwar
Art Editor Emma Hobson
Freelance Designer Radhika Banerjee
Jacket Editor Francesca Young
Jacket Designer Amy Keast
DTP Designers Nand Kishor Acharya, Nityanand Kumar, Dheeraj Singh
Picture Researcher Sakshi Saluja
Producer, Pre-Production Nadine King
Senior Producer Srijana Gurung
Managing Editors Soma B. Chowdhury, Laura Gilbert
Managing Art Editors Neha Ahuja Chowdhry, Diane Peyton Jones
Art Director Martin Wilson
Publisher Sarah Larter

Reading Consultant
Linda Gambrell, Ph.D.
Subject Consultant
Janelle Gendrano

First American Edition, 2017
Published in the United States by DK Publishing
345 Hudson Street, New York, New York 10014

Copyright © 2017 Dorling Kindersley Limited
DK, a Division of Penguin Random House LLC
17 18 19 20 21 10 9 8 7 6 5 4 3 2 1
001—298970—January/17

A catalog record for this book is available from the Library of Congress.

ISBN: 978-1-4654-5748-6 (Paperback)
ISBN: 978-1-4654-5749-3 (Hardcover)

DK books are available at special discounts when purchased in bulk for sales promotions,
premiums, fund-raising, or educational use. For details, contact:
DK Publishing Special Markets
345 Hudson Street, New York, New York 10014
SpecialSales@dk.com

Printed and bound in China.

The publisher would also like to thank the following for their kind permission
to reproduce their photographs:
(Key: a=above, b=below/bottom, c=center, l=left, r=right, t=top)
4 123RF.com: Alan Cotton (b). **5 123RF.com:** Visions of America LLC. **6 Dreamstime.com:** Georgios Kollidas (b).
7 123RF.com: petervick167 (tl). **Rex by Shutterstock:** Courtesy Everett Collection (tr); Globe Photos (bl); Nara Archives
(br). **8–9 Dreamstime.com:** Americanspirit. **10–11 Getty Images:** Hirz / Archive Photos. **12–13 123RF.com:** rudi1976
(Background). **12 123RF.com:** Richard Laschon (c). **13 123RF.com:** experimental (crb). **iStockphoto.com:** YasyaPetra (tl).
16 123RF.com: Rolando Da Jose (cl). **18–19 Dreamstime.com:** Alberto Dubini. **20 Rex by Shutterstock:** White House (b).
21 Alamy Stock Photo: White House Photo. **22–23 123RF.com:** rudi1976 (Background). **22 Alamy Stock Photo:**
White House Photo. **23 Alamy Stock Photo:** White House Photo (b). **Getty Images:** Greg Mathieson / Mai / Mai / The Life
Images (t). **24–25 Alamy Stock Photo:** Everett Collection Inc. **26–27 Dreamstime.com:** Eleu Tabares (t). **27 Alamy Stock
Photo:** Mark Thomas (b). **28–29 Getty Images:** Diana Walker / / Time Life Pictures. **30–31 Alamy Stock Photo:** Everett
Collection Inc. **32–33 123RF.com:** rudi1976 (Background). **34 Alamy Stock Photo:** Everett Collection Historical (b).
34–35 Getty Images: David E. Klutho / Sports Illustrated. **36–37 Alamy Stock Photo:** dpa picture alliance.
38–39 Alamy Stock Photo: EPA / Dean Forbes. **40–41 Alamy Stock Photo:** White House Photo. **42 123RF.com:** rudi1976 (Background). **SuperStock:** Ping Amranand / Ping Amranand
Jacket images: _Front:_ **Alamy Stock Photo:** Niday Picture Library clb, RGB Ventures / SuperStock cb/ (Lincoln),
Stuwdamdorp; **Getty Images:** Pete Souza / The White House cb, Universal History Archive crb

All other images © Dorling Kindersley
For further information see: www.dkimages.com

A WORLD OF IDEAS:
SEE ALL THERE IS TO KNOW
www.dk.com

Contents

Words in **bold** appear in the glossary.

Chapter 1
The President

The president of the United States of America is the leader of the country. Being the president is a very important job.

The Presidential Seal is the official symbol of the president of the United States. It shows an American bald eagle and 50 stars for the 50 states.

Barack Obama
44th president of the United States, 2009–2017

Every four years, **citizens** of the United States **vote** to choose their president. Americans must be at least 18 years old to vote. They vote for the person who they think will do the best job.

These are some past presidents.

George Washington
1st president, 1789–1797

Abraham Lincoln
16th president, 1861–1865

Franklin D. Roosevelt
32nd president, 1933–1945

John F. Kennedy
35th president, 1961–1963

George H.W. Bush
41st president, 1989–1993

If you want to become president, first you need to **campaign**. This means asking people to vote for you in the **election**.

You need to tell people what
you would do for the country
if you were president.

Bill Clinton campaigns
in 1996.

The person who wins the election becomes president of the United States.

Abraham Lincoln takes the oath of office in 1861. The oath of office is the promise made by every new president to do what is best for the United States.

The new president must
promise to do what is best
for the country.

Do you want to run for president?

You need to have lived in the United States for at least 14 years.

You must have been
born a citizen of
the United States.

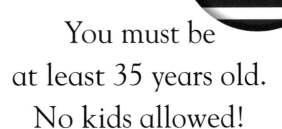

You must be
at least 35 years old.
No kids allowed!

13

Chapter 2
Washington, D.C.

WASHINGTON

MONTANA

OREGON

IDAHO

WYOMING

ALASKA

NEVADA

CALIFORNIA

UTAH

COLORAD

ARIZONA

NEW
MEXICO

HAWAII

The president lives in Washington, D.C. It is the capital city of the United States of America.

This map shows the United States of America. The capital city, Washington, D.C., is marked with a star.

The United States **government** is located in Washington, D.C. The city was named after the first president of the United States, George Washington.

The Washington Monument was built in honor of George Washington.

There are many **monuments** that honor past presidents in Washington, D.C.

This statue of Abraham Lincoln is part of the Lincoln Memorial.

The president's home is the White House. It has been home to every American president—except one!

George Washington didn't live in the White House. It was still being built when he was president!

The White House in Washington, D.C.

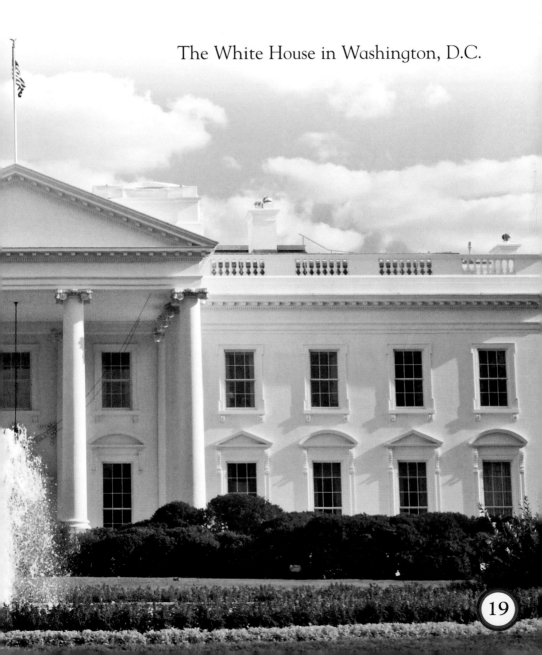

The president's family lives in the White House, too. The White House has 132 rooms, so there's plenty of space to live, work, and play.

John F. Kennedy watches his children, Caroline and John, play in the White House in 1962.

Barack and Michelle Obama pose with their daughters, Malia and Sasha, and their dogs, Sunny and Bo, outside the White House in 2015.

Let's explore the White House!

The president's main office is the Oval Office.

The president meets official staff in the
Cabinet Room.

Bedrooms for the president's family and guests
are upstairs.

Chapter 3
A Hard Job

Ronald Reagan at work in 1982

A good president tries to do what is right for the American people. The president has to make some tough decisions.

Air Force One—the president's airplane

The president often travels on *Air Force One* to meet leaders of other countries. They try to find ways for our world to live in peace.

Barack Obama with British Prime Minister
David Cameron in London, England, in 2016

The president is in charge of
the American **armed forces**.

The armed forces keep Americans safe.

George H. W. Bush with US soldiers in Saudi Arabia in 1990

The president works with Congress to decide on the **laws** for the country. Congress is made up of people elected from the 50 states.

IN GOD WE TRUST

Jimmy Carter speaks to Congress in 1978.

The US Congress

- Congress is made up of the Senate and the House of Representatives.

- There are 100 senators in the Senate. Each state has two senators.

- There are 435 representatives in the House of Representatives. States with a lot of people have more representatives than states with fewer people.

The Capitol building in Washington, D.C., is where Congress meets.

★★★★★★★★★★★★★★★★★★★

Chapter 4
Exciting Times

★★★★★★★★★★★★★★★★★★★

Being president is hard work, but it is exciting, too! There are lots of fun **traditions**.

Franklin D. Roosevelt throws a baseball at an All-Star Game in 1937.

Barack Obama throws the first pitch at the 2009 Major League Baseball All-Star Game.

The president hosts fun events at the White House, such as the Fourth of July barbecue.

The president also gives awards,
such as the Medal of Freedom,
to people who do great things.

Barack Obama hosts a Fourth of July
barbecue at the White House in 2013.

THE GRANITE STATE
ROCK SOLID FOR BUSH

The president meets many people and listens to what they think the country needs. The president also gives lots of speeches. Imagine the whole country listening to what you have to say!

George W. Bush speaks to people in New Hampshire in 2004.

The president works for the American people. They count on the president to do what is right for the country. It is an important job!

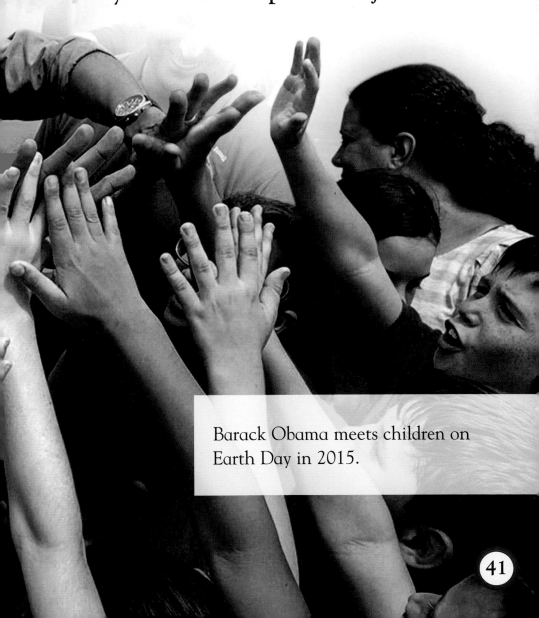

Barack Obama meets children on Earth Day in 2015.

Would you like to be the president of the United States?

What would you do for the country?

The President's Quiz

1. How often do Americans vote to choose their president?

2. What is the capital city of the United States?

3. What is the president's house called?

4. What is the president's main office called?

5. Who does the president work with to decide on the laws for the country?

Answers on page 45.

Glossary

armed forces
the military organization that protects the country

campaign
when a person who is running in an election asks for votes

citizens
people who are legally part of a country

election
when people vote for who they want to be in charge

government
group of people who run a city, state, or country by making decisions for its people

laws

rules of a country or state that people live by

monuments

statues or buildings that honor someone or something

traditions

events that have been celebrated in the same way for many years

vote

to choose a person you think should win an election

Answers to The President's Quiz:

1. Every four years **2.** Washington, D.C.
3. The White House **4.** The Oval Office
5. Congress

Guide for Parents

This book is part of an exciting four-level reading series for children, developing the habit of reading widely for both pleasure and information. These chapter books have a compelling main narrative to suit your child's reading ability. Each book is designed to develop your child's reading skills, fluency, grammar awareness, and comprehension in order to build confidence and engagement when reading.

Ready for a *Level 2* book

YOUR CHILD SHOULD

- be familiar with using beginning letter sounds and context clues to figure out unfamiliar words.
- be aware of the need for a slight pause at commas and a longer one at periods.
- alter his/her expression for questions and exclamations.

A VALUABLE AND SHARED READING EXPERIENCE

For many children, reading requires much effort, but adult participation can make this both fun and easier. So here are a few tips on how to use this book with your child.

TIP 1 Check out the contents together before your child begins:

- read the text about the book on the back cover.
- flip through the book and stop to chat about the contents page together to heighten your child's interest and expectation.
- make use of unfamiliar or difficult words on the page in a brief discussion.
- chat about the nonfiction reading features used in the book, such as headings, captions, lists, or charts.

TIP 2 Support your child as he/she reads the story pages:

- give the book to your child to read and turn the pages.

- where necessary, encourage your child to break a word into syllables, sound out each one, and then flow the syllables together. Ask him/her to reread the sentence to check the meaning.

- when there's a question mark or an exclamation mark, encourage your child to vary his/her voice as he/she reads the sentence. Demonstrate how to do this if it is helpful.

TIP 3 Chat at the end of each page:

- ask questions about the text and the meaning of the words used. These help to develop comprehension skills and awareness of the language used.

A FEW ADDITIONAL TIPS

- Always encourage your child to try reading difficult words by himself/herself. Praise any self-corrections, for example, "I like the way you sounded out that word and then changed the way you said it, to make sense."

- Try to read together every day. Reading little and often is best. These books are divided into manageable chapters for one reading session. However, after 10 minutes, only keep going if your child wants to read on.

- Read other books of different types to your child just for enjoyment and information.

Series consultant, **Dr. Linda Gambrell**, Distinguished Professor of Education at Clemson University, has served as President of the National Reading Conference, the College Reading Association, and the International Reading Association.

Index